A Congress WBN Publication

Produced By:

 and

DISCOVERING God TOGETHER

Discovery Workbook #8

THIS BOOK BELONGS TO:

_____

About the WE MAGNIFY YOU Discovery Workbook Series

Our families are at the core of our Kingdom Communities. The WE MAGNIFY YOU album provides us with a wonderful opportunity to develop and strengthen the expression of worship in our homes.

Each We Magnify You Discovery Workbook has been designed for parents, guardians, teachers and children to experience and explore the songs together.

Discover new sight of what it means to magnify, exalt and praise our God. Together, our families will develop a deeper and stronger understanding of who God is, releasing a whole-hearted expression of worship unto Him.

For each song on the WE MAGNIFY YOU album, we have a Workbook with the lyrics and specially created activities.

Enjoy taking time together to consider what the lyrics mean. Explore scripture verses that tell us more about each song. Engage in fun activities, including word puzzles and coloring games.

Through it all we can together gain a deeper understanding of how the words we sing reflect the lives we must live, as we align ourselves to God.

Now that is a beautiful thing!

Guidance for Parents

The WE MAGNIFY YOU worship album from Congress MusicFactory contains prayers and songs from Dr. Woodroffe and saints from Elijah Centre and Kingdom Communities across Congress WBN.

WE MAGNIFY YOU is a powerful expression of worship and praise to our Lord. Each workbook in the We Magnify You Discovery Series explores the lyrics of the songs, sharing explanations, key scriptures and fun activities.

These resources will help us to align our lives, our families and our communities to the words that we lift unto God.

AMEN!

LYRICS

You are the God of all creation
All things are under Your command
Bring Your judgment to the nations
Cause Your righteous ones to stand

Amen!
So let it be!
Amen!
Hear our decree!
Let Your Kingdom come
Lord let Your will be done
Now and forevermore
Amen!

Send Your word throughout the nations
Let Your chosen hear Your call
Make us one, Your holy people
Reveal Your glory now to all

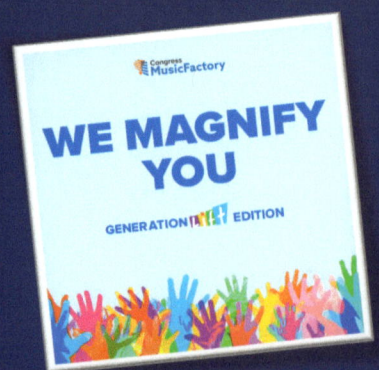

WE MAGNIFY YOU Discovery Workbook Series

Activity Time

Your Kingdom come, Your will be done, on earth as it is in Heaven.

Matthew 6:10

The word **Amen** is actually derived from the Hebrew ā mēn, which means "surely" or "truth". It's a word used to communicate certainty and agreement.

When we declare, **"Amen!"** we are telling God that we agree with His plans and want them to happen!

Decree is another word for declaration or command. A command is given by someone with the right, power or authority to communicate it. As God's children, we have been given the right and authority to make **decrees** on His behalf.

"Hear our decree!" is us telling God to pay attention to us because we agree with His will and we are prepared to help Him to fulfill it.

We have authority - given to us by God - to make decrees. What we decree on earth will be decreed in Heaven.

Jesus says
"I will give you the keys to the Kingdom of Heaven.
What you lock on earth will be locked in Heaven.
What you unlock on earth will be unlocked in Heaven."
Matthew 16: 19

Use the keys below to unlock the padlocks! Draw a line from each key to the padlock it fits:

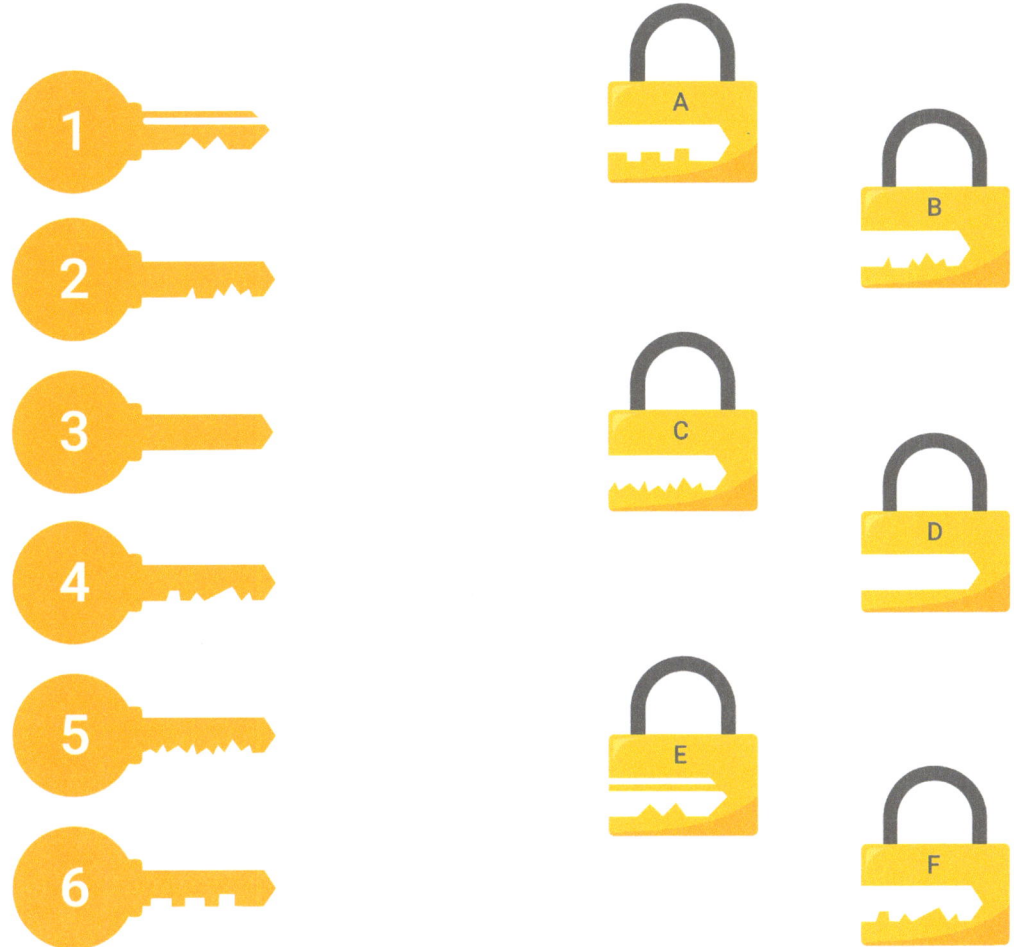

BOOK 8: Amen

When we say, **"Let Your Kingdom come, let Your will be done,"** we are making a decree to the heavens and the earth of our desire to see His laws, His ways and His purpose expressed in our lives.

A kingdom is ruled by a king. Whenever we accept the will of God and obey His command we make Him the King of our life. And when He is the King of our life, His Kingdom come, in us and in the earth – cause that's where we live!

Now and forevermore - tells us that we want everything that God wants, today and always.

"... behold, the kingdom of God is within you."
Luke 17:21

Color the meanings of the word Amen

Activity Time

What does Amen mean?
So Let it be
I AGREE!

CERTAINLY!

I AGREE!

LET IT BE!

SO BE IT!

THAT'S TRUE!

YES!

BOOK 8: Amen

A CLOSER LOOK

You are the God of all creation
All things are under Your command

Everything in the world was created by God.

In the book of Genesis in the Bible He commanded the world in to existence.

We are part of God's creation and our job is to do all that He commands!

God made all the things we see, and even things that are way too small to see!

By the word of the Lord the heavens were made,
And all the host of them by the breath of His mouth...

Psalm 33:6

Color the picture.
- How many fish can you count?
- How many starfish can you spot?
- Do you see any other sea-creatures?

Job 12:10

It is God who directs the lives of His creatures, everyone's life is in His power.

DID YOU KNOW: God knows how many fish swim in the sea and how many birds fly in the air—all of creation is under His command!

BOOK 8: Amen

A CLOSER LOOK

Bring Your judgment to the nations

At the Finish, God will judge all people.

This means that He will reward those who love and obey Him and punish those who do not.

You can be sure that I live forever.
And you can be just as sure that I will sharpen my flashing sword.
My hand will hold it when I judge.
I will get even with my enemies.
I will pay back those who hate Me.

Deuteronomy 32: 40-41

As God's children, we have the right to make declarations or decrees on His behalf!

Fill in the blanks with the missing words from the song.

_____ So let it be

You are the God of all _____

Make us one Your _____ people

Bring Your _____ to the nations

BOOK 8: Amen

We are God's **righteous ones** because we walk in His ways, doing what is right in His eyes.

Let's ask the Holy Spirit to continue to help us to walk faithfully with God, so that our actions and choices will always show God that He is important to us!

> *Arise, shine, for your light has come, and the glory of the Lord rises upon you.*
>
> *Isaiah 60:1*

Find these words from the song hidden in the puzzle below:

☐ CREATION ☐ AMEN ☐ DECREE

☐ COMMAND ☐ STAND ☐ JUDGEMENT

☐ RIGHTEOUS ☐ KINGDOM

T	C	O	M	M	A	N	D	S	D	G	A	A	T
T	O	A	R	I	G	H	T	E	O	U	S	S	M
E	E	D	N	K	I	N	G	D	O	M	T	E	T
J	J	A	I	S	E	N	N	R	A	I	C	O
A	D	A	N	M	N	E	T	M	N	N	H	R	E
I	R	N	G	N	S	M	T	D	E	M	E	E	A
E	M	D	A	N	E	A	H	S	M	M	N	A	I
N	U	D	E	A	I	M	I	M	S	S	A	T	T
J	G	I	E	N	I	C	N	C	D	G	T	I	S
O	O	R	M	C	T	S	G	G	D	A	I	O	O
D	G	N	N	J	R	E	S	O	A	D	O	N	A
I	I	A	N	T	N	E	A	S	N	N	N	U	S
E	C	O	N	E	O	S	E	U	S	N	S	N	M
H	R	E	N	A	S	T	S	E	O	U	E	G	G

BOOK 8: Amen

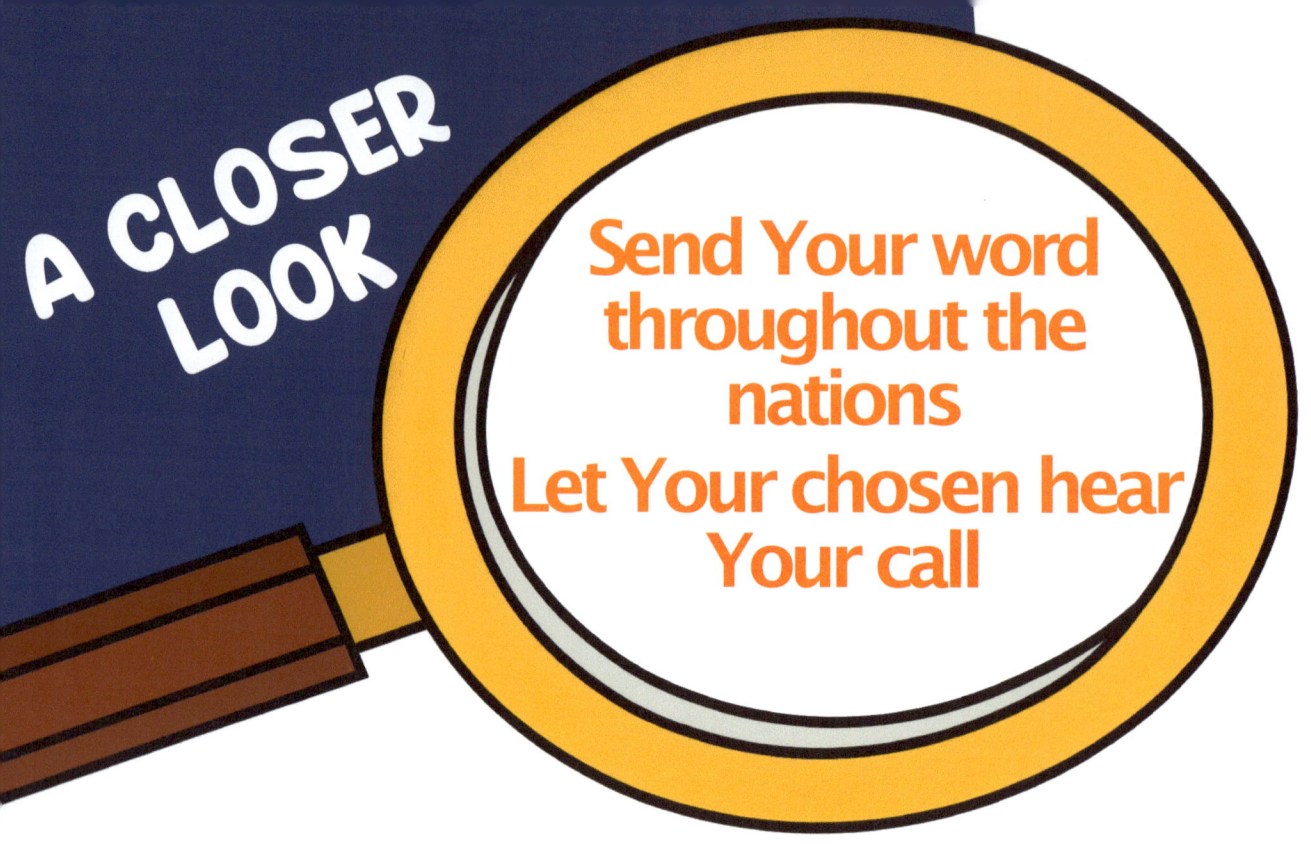

One of the final commands that Jesus gave to His disciples was to go out to the nations and spread the word of the Lord.

We partner with God to:

- Declare His will for the Earth

- Call His chosen people into His Kingdom

- Set an example for all nations to see His Glory, mercy and goodness by the way we live our lives.

Match the scrambled words to their solution:

EEDREC • • COMMAND

ONCRAITE • • NATIONS

MMODANC • • CHOSEN

NASNIOT • • PEOPLE

NSDTA • • GLORY

SHNOEC • • DECREE

LEPEOP • • CREATION

LGRYO • • STAND

**Make us one Your Holy People
Reveal Your glory now to all**

Oneness and Holiness are very, very, very, important to God. So, we sing this to let Him know that we need His help to **make us one, His holy people.**

When we dwell together in perfect harmony, together as one, we show the world exactly what God is like – Father, Son and Holy Spirit working together as one.

When the world sees that in us, God's glory is revealed. How amazing! What an incredible job we have to do together - to reveal the Glory of God to the entire earth!

Draw faces and clothes on the people, and color them in to help you remember we are **ONE** as God's people across the globe.

Activity Time

For you are a chosen people. You are royal priests, a holy nation, God's very own possession. As a result, you can show others the goodness of God.

1 Peter 2:9

BOOK 8: Amen

Take some time to reflect on this song. Here's some space to write down your thoughts.

MY JOURNAL

www.ingramcontent.com/pod-product-compliance
Lightning Source LLC
Chambersburg PA
CBHW041123070526
44584CB00002B/255